An Alphabet

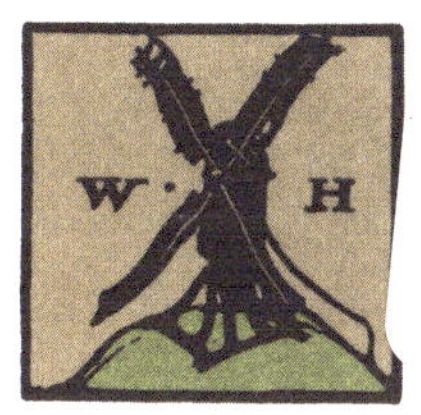

By William Nicholson

Published by William Heinemann. London
1898.

An Alphabet

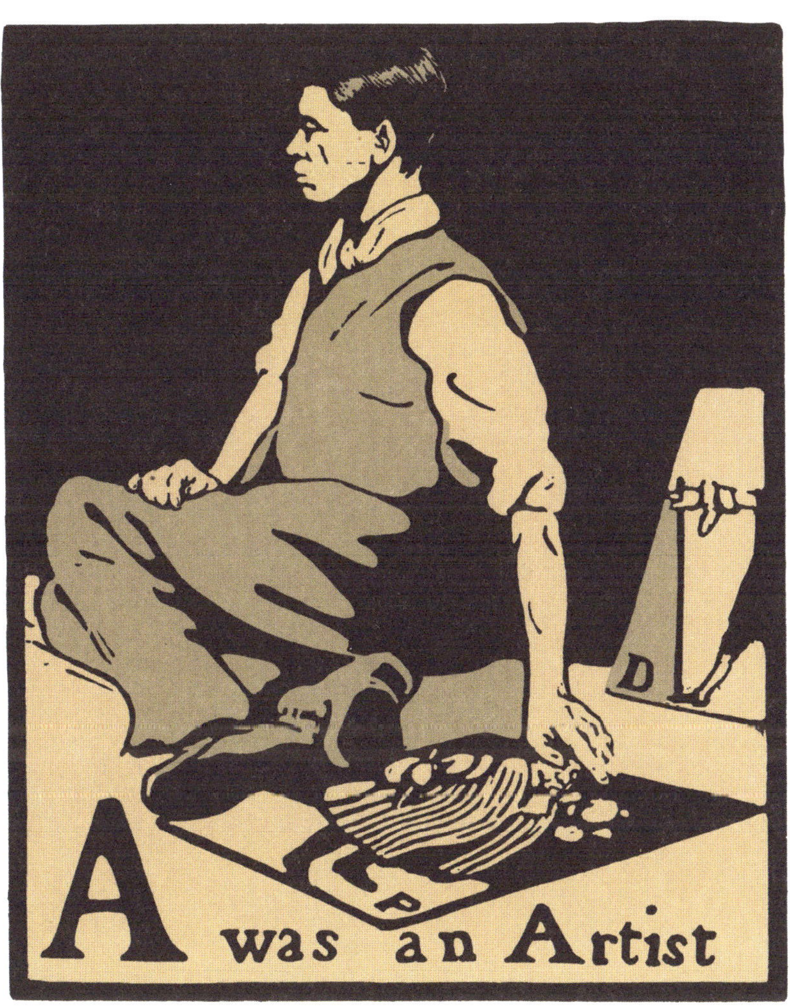
D
P
A was an Artist

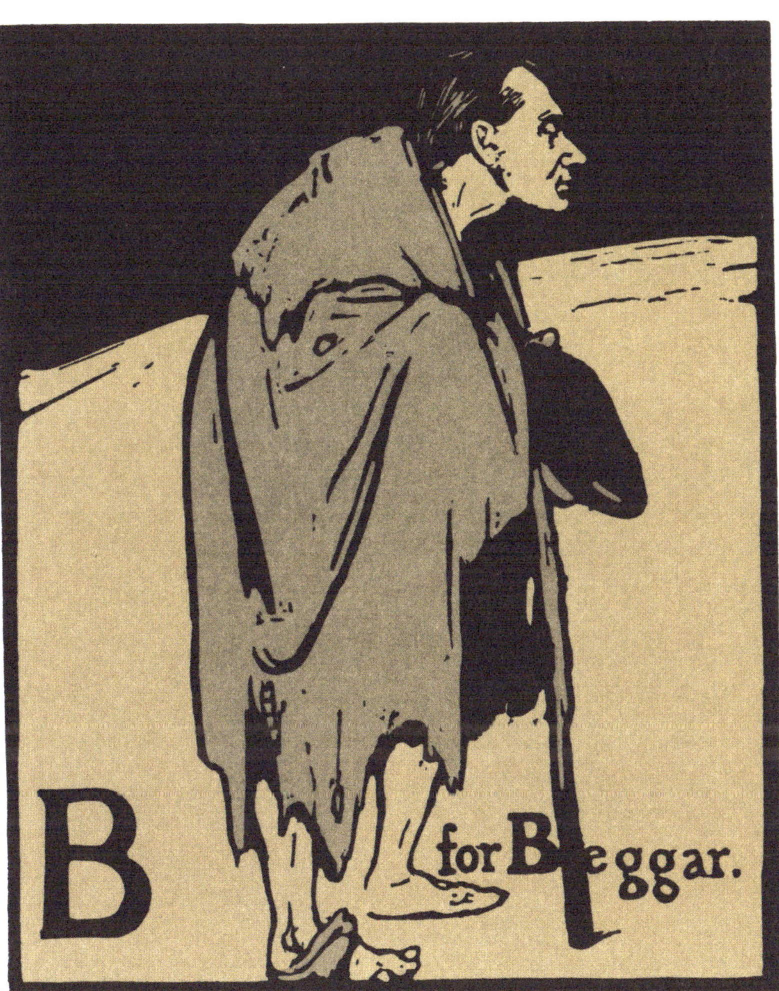
B for Beggar.

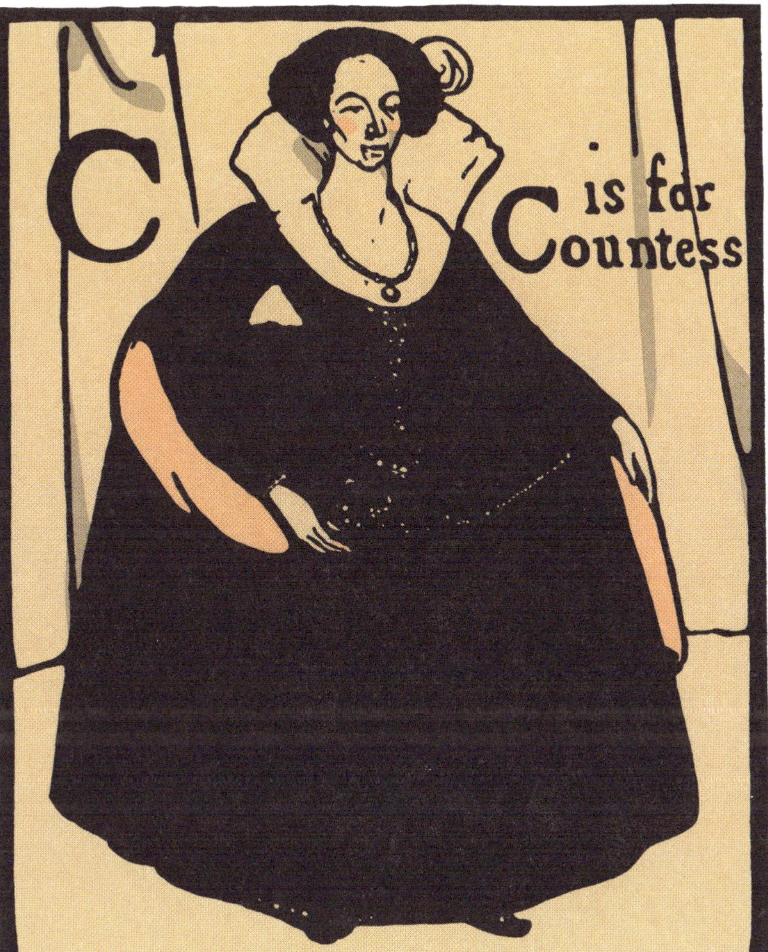
C
C is for Countess

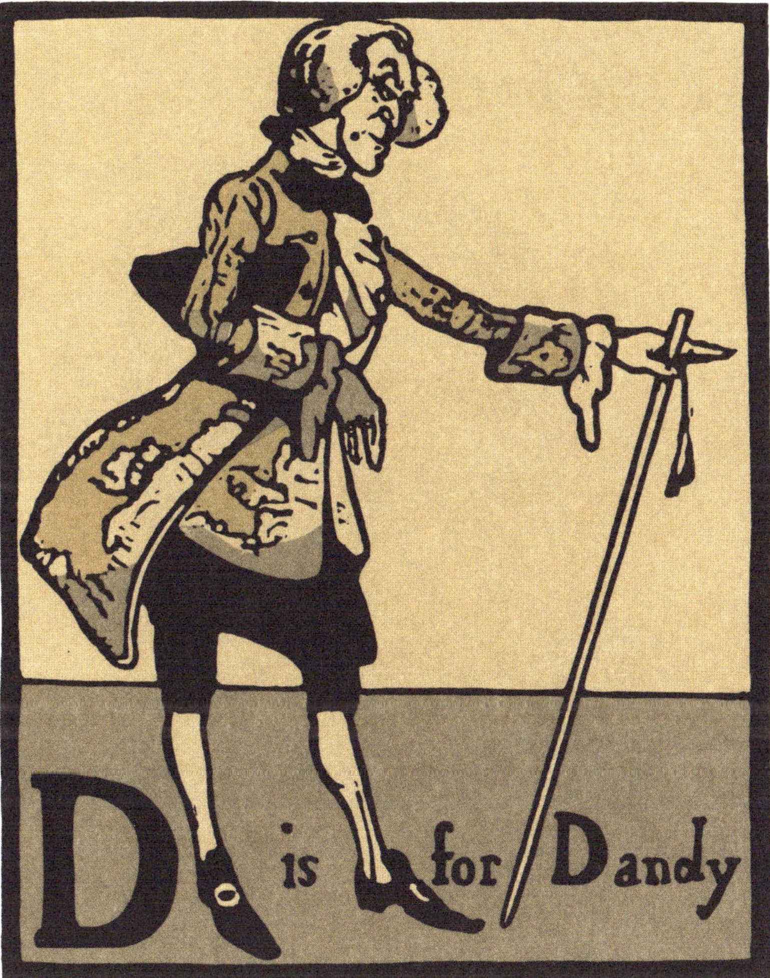
D is for Dandy

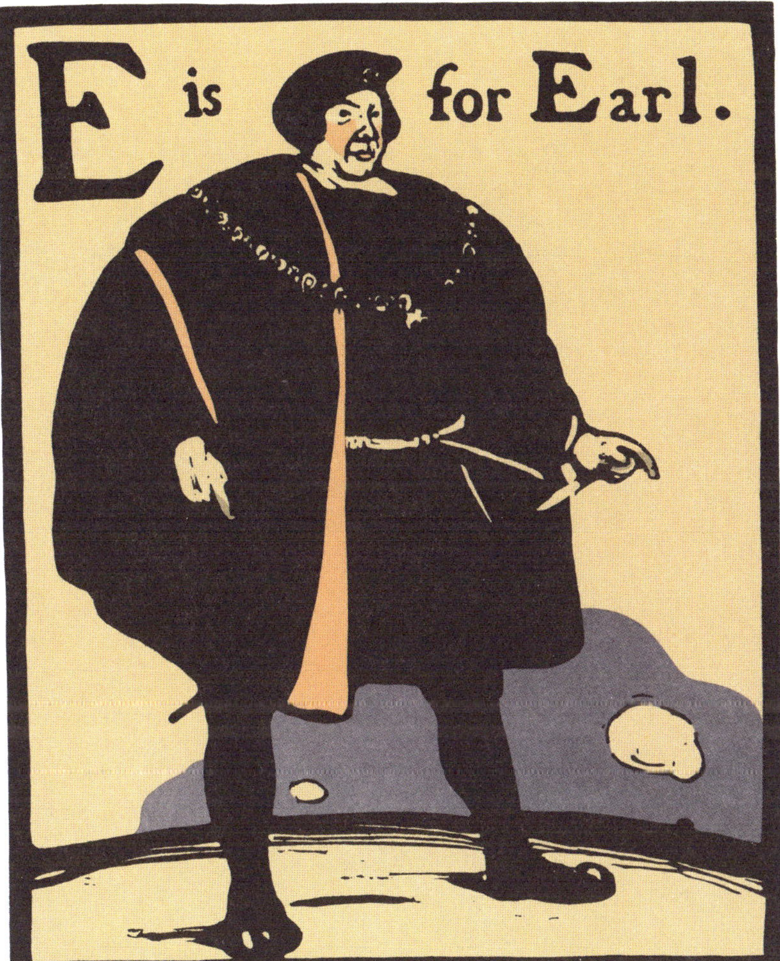
E is for Earl.

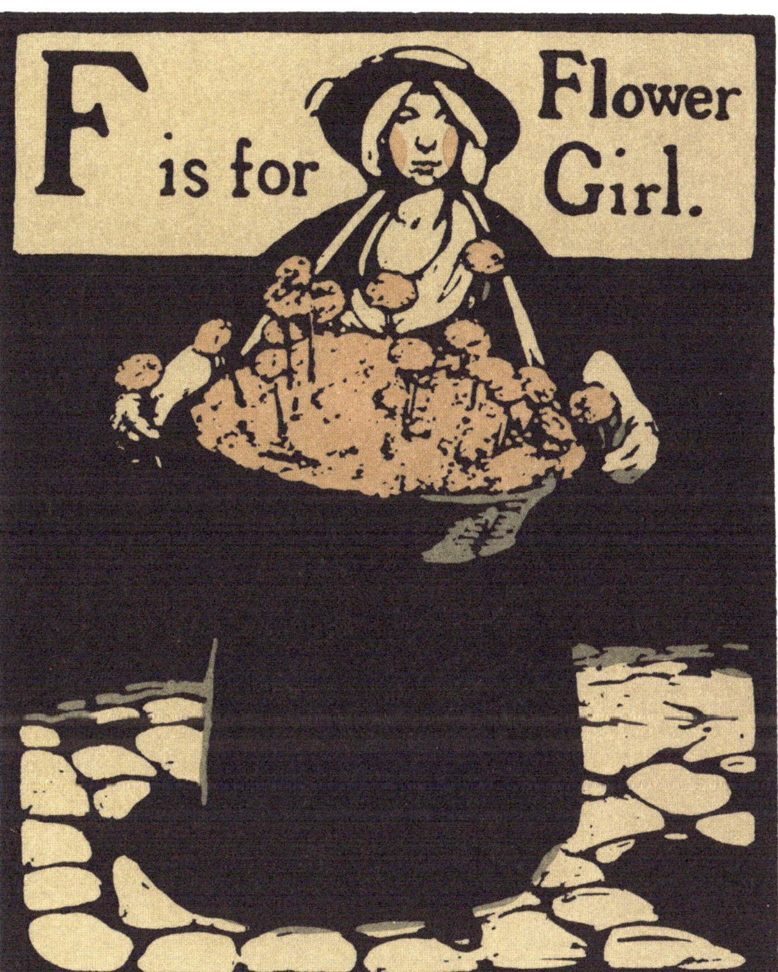
F is for
Flower
Girl.

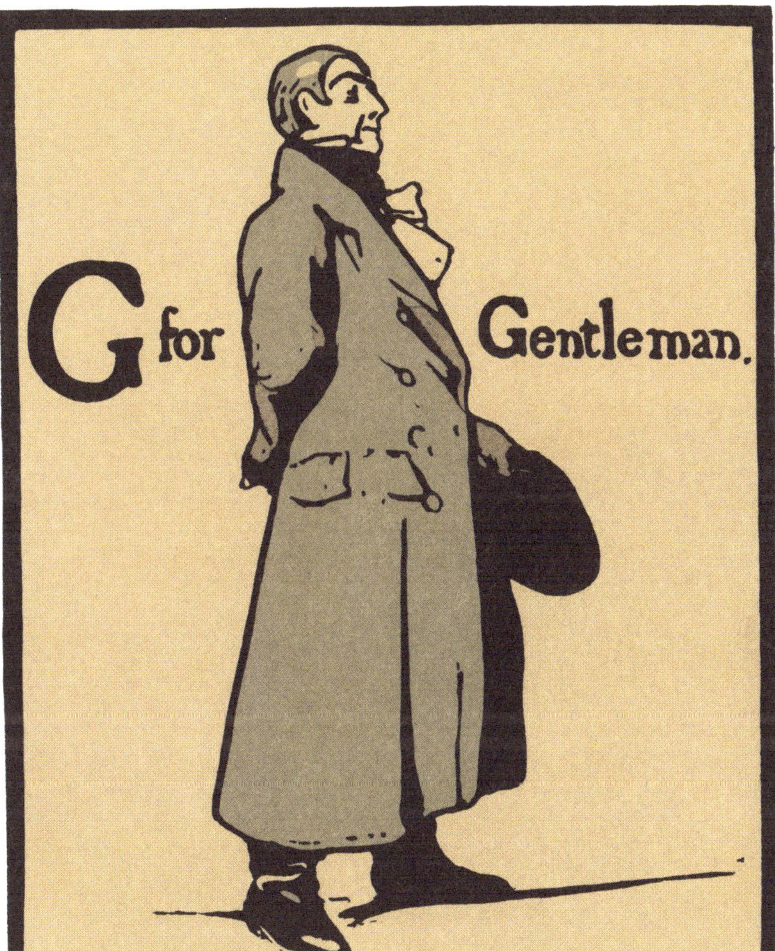
G for Gentleman.

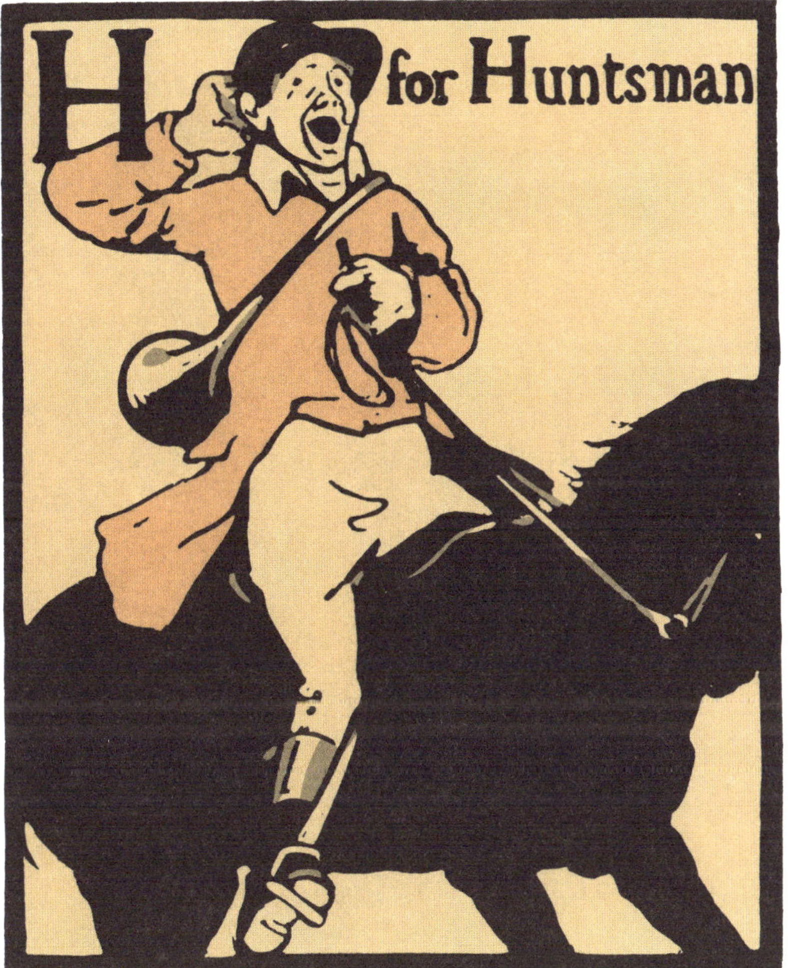
H for Huntsman

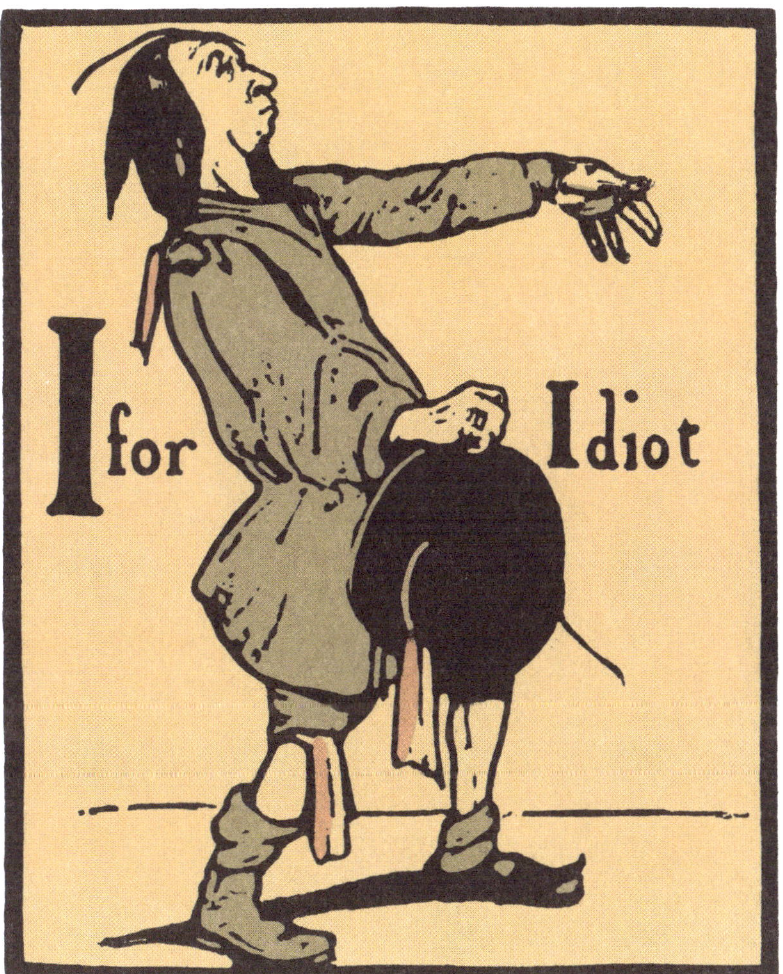
I for Idiot

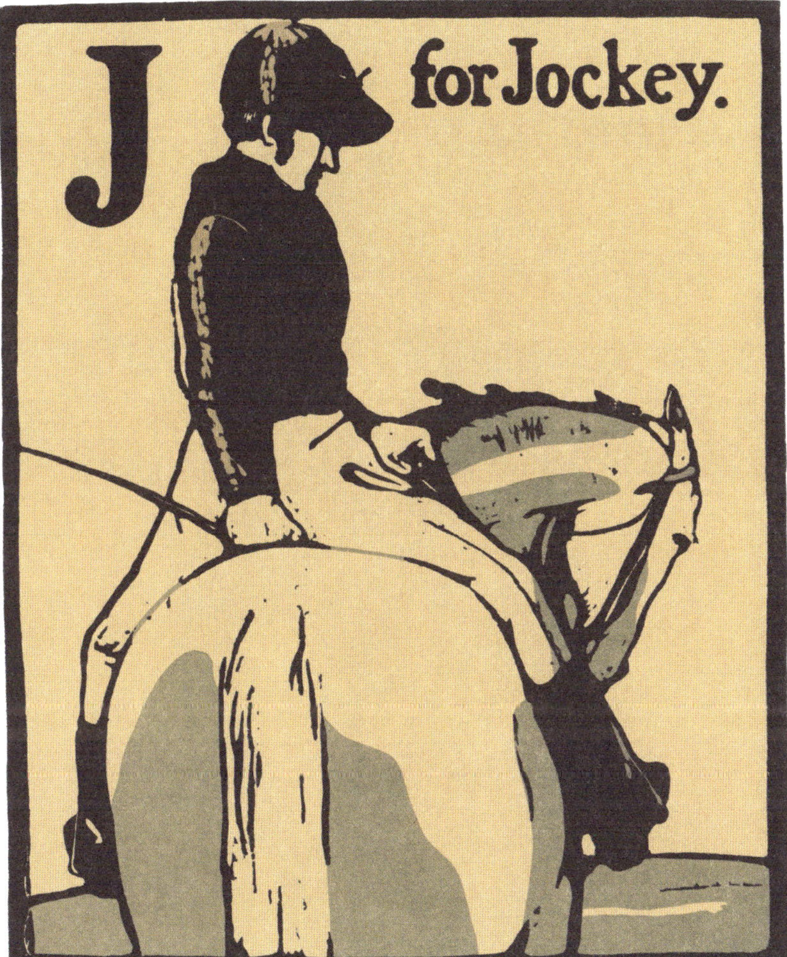
J for Jockey.

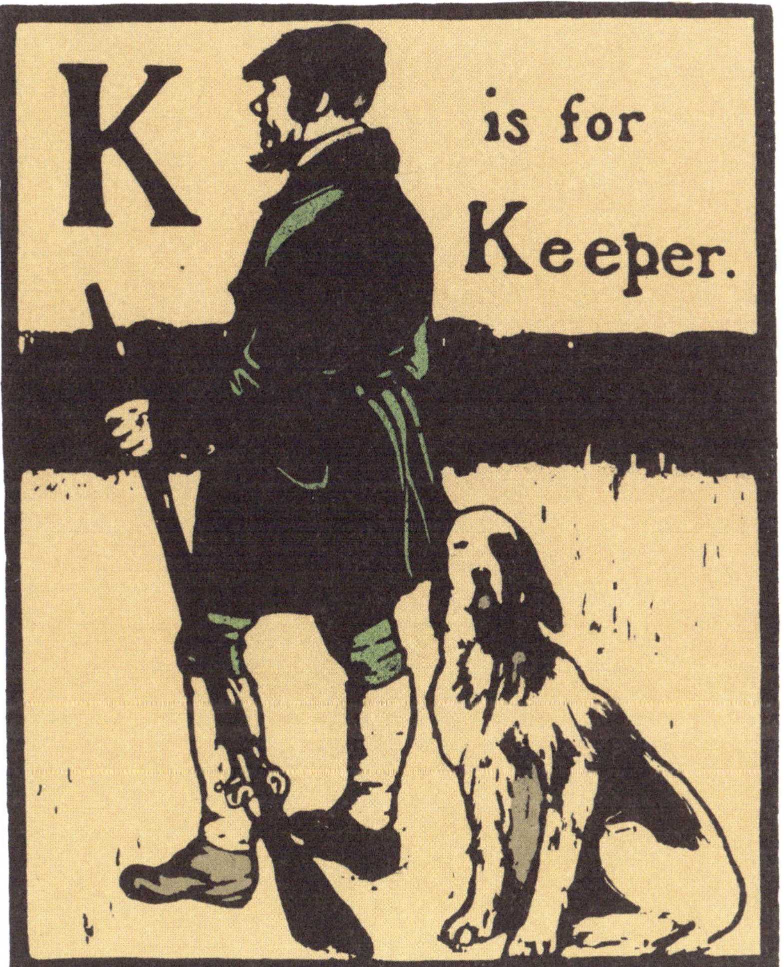
K is for Keeper.

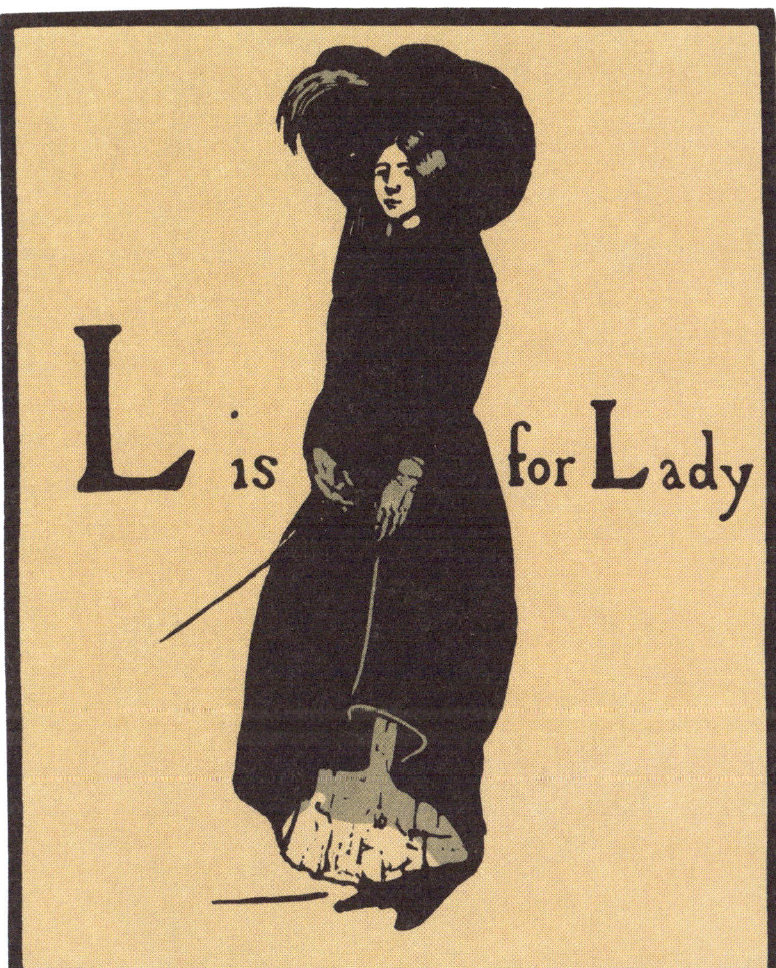
L is for Lady

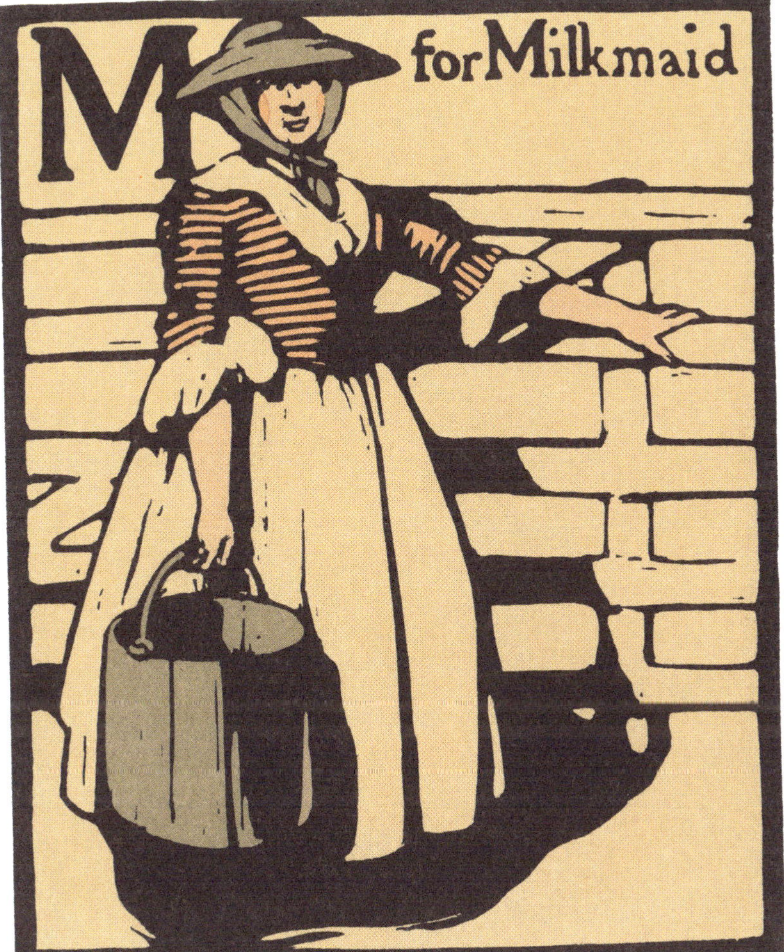
M for Milkmaid

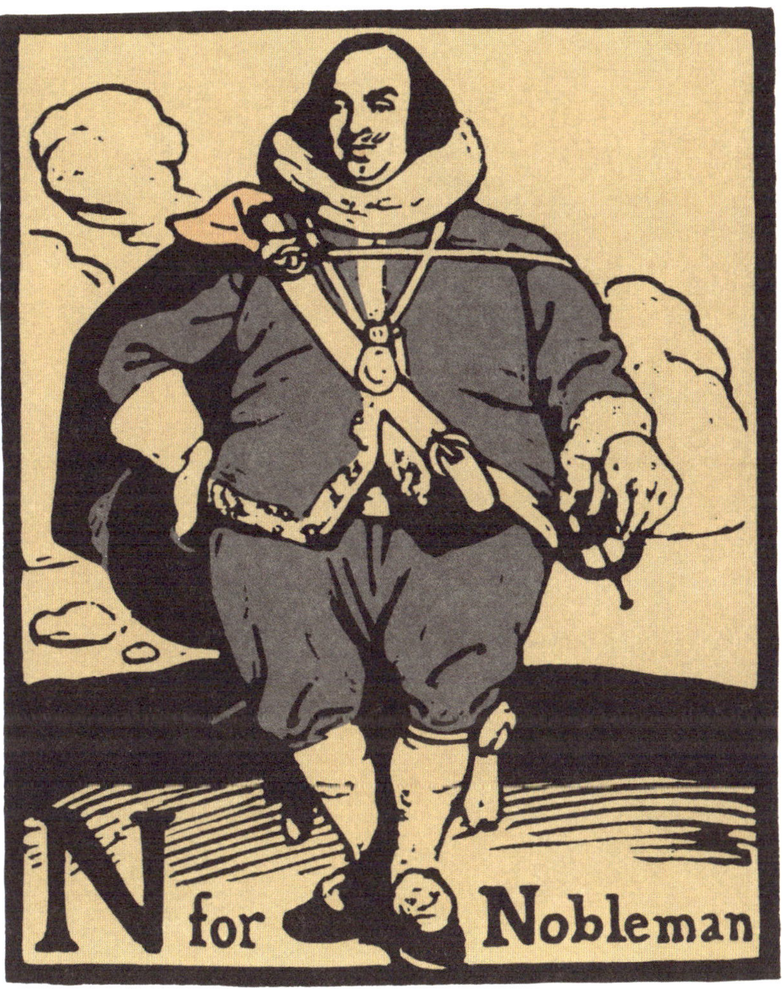
N for Nobleman

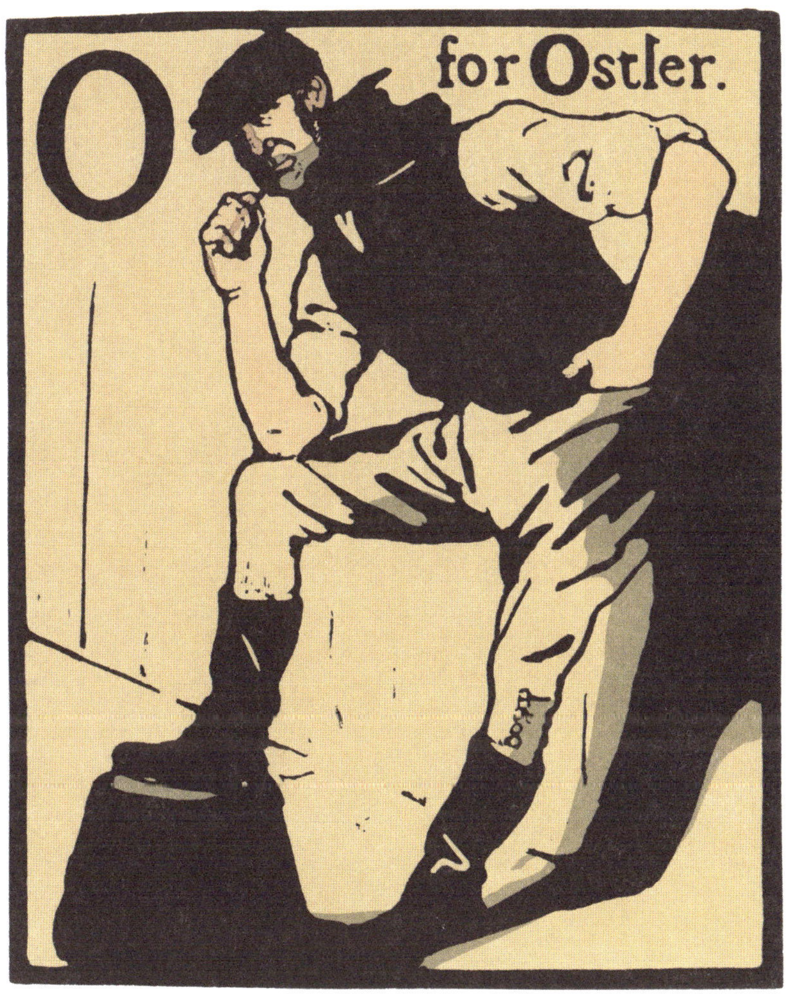
O for Ostler.

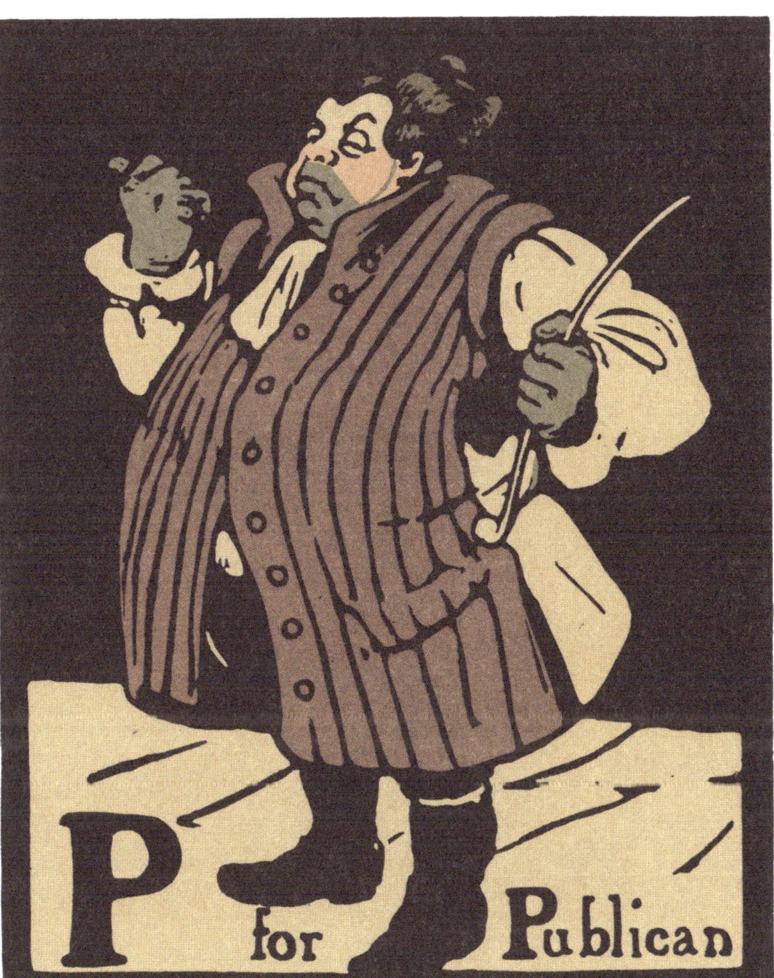
P for Publican

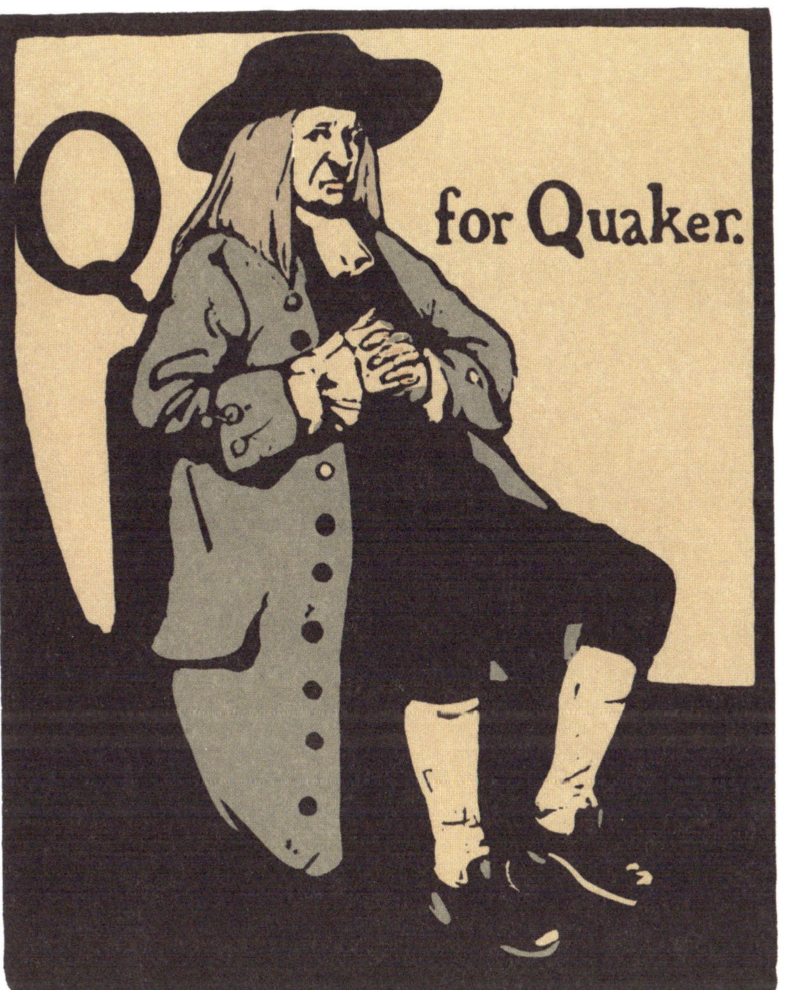
Q
for Quaker.

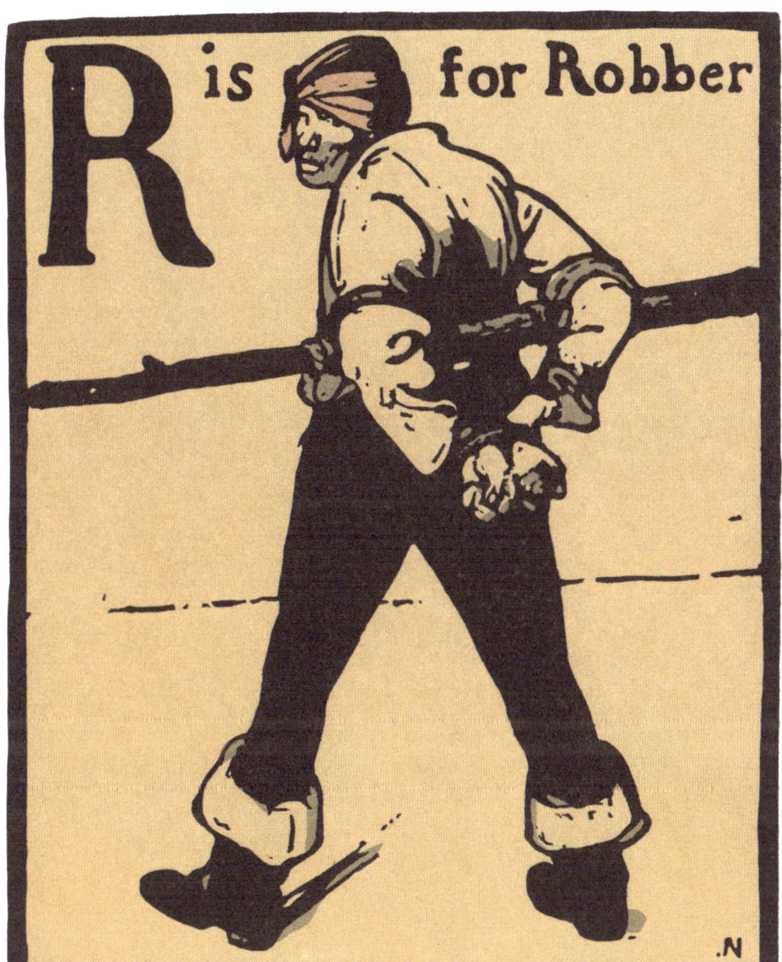
R is for Robber
N

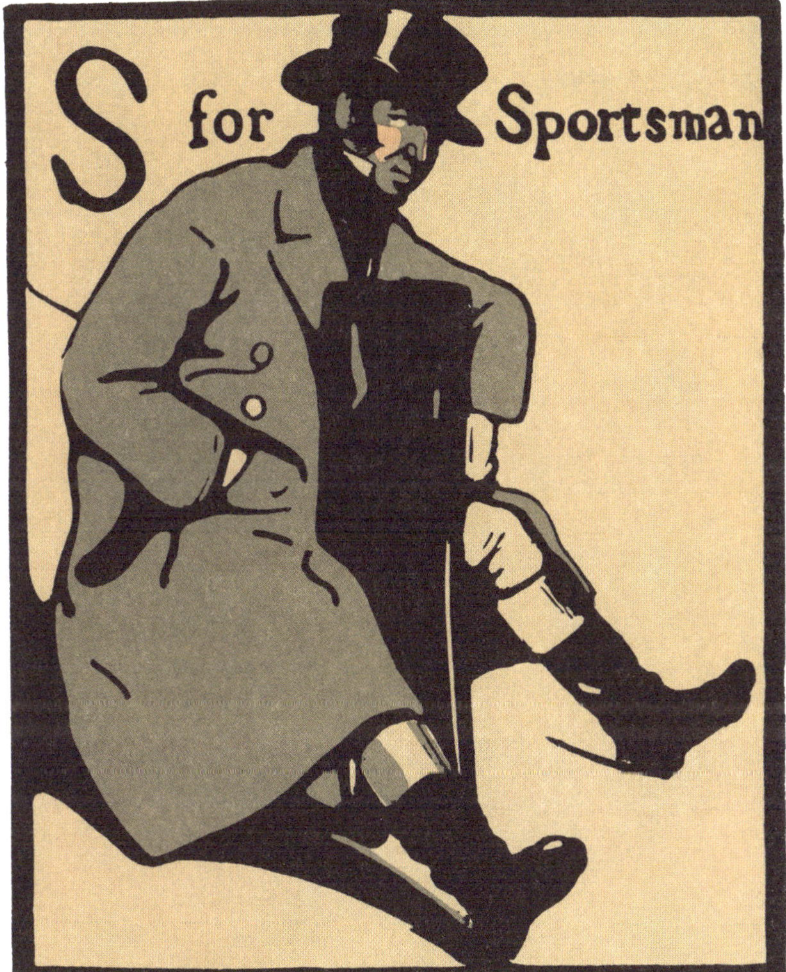
S for Sportsman

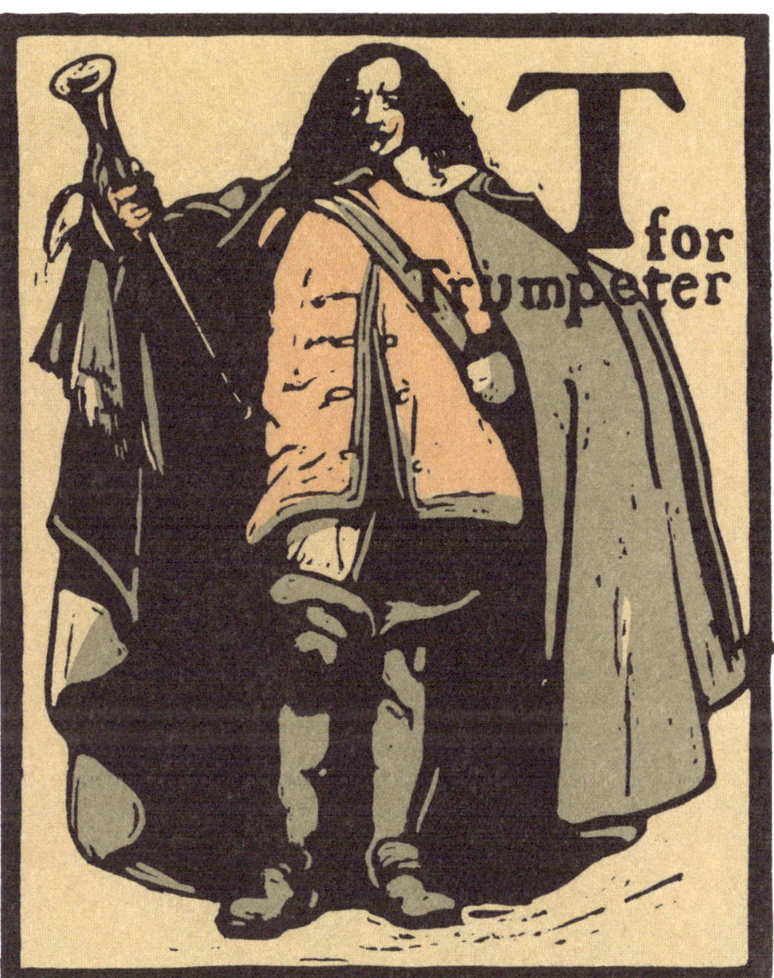
T for Trumpeter

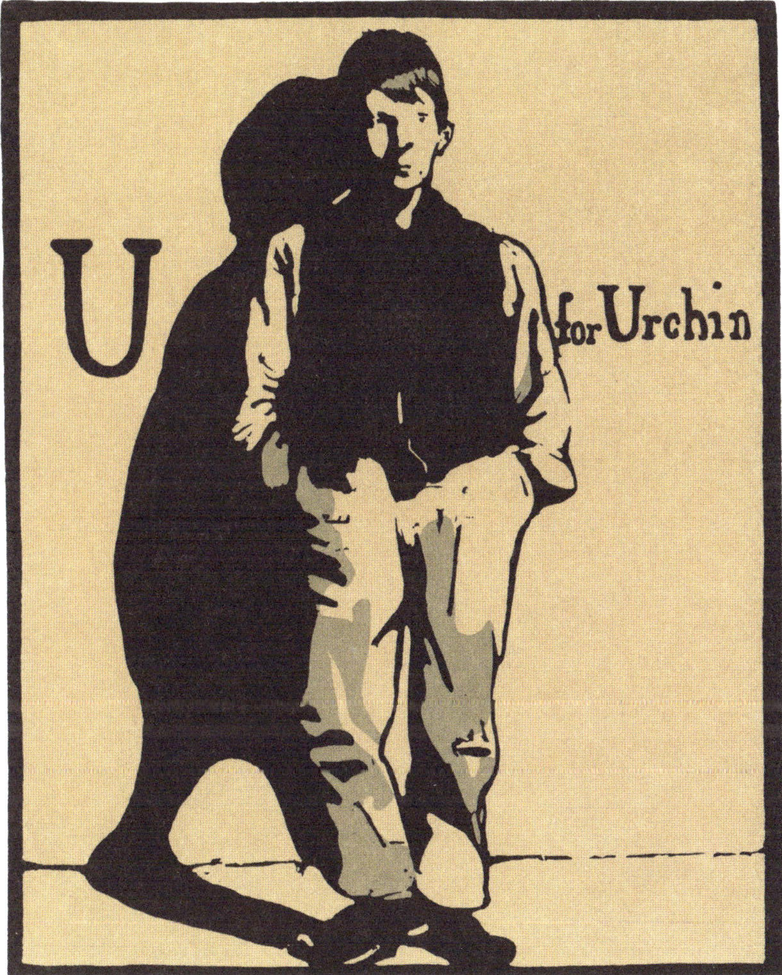
U
for Urchin

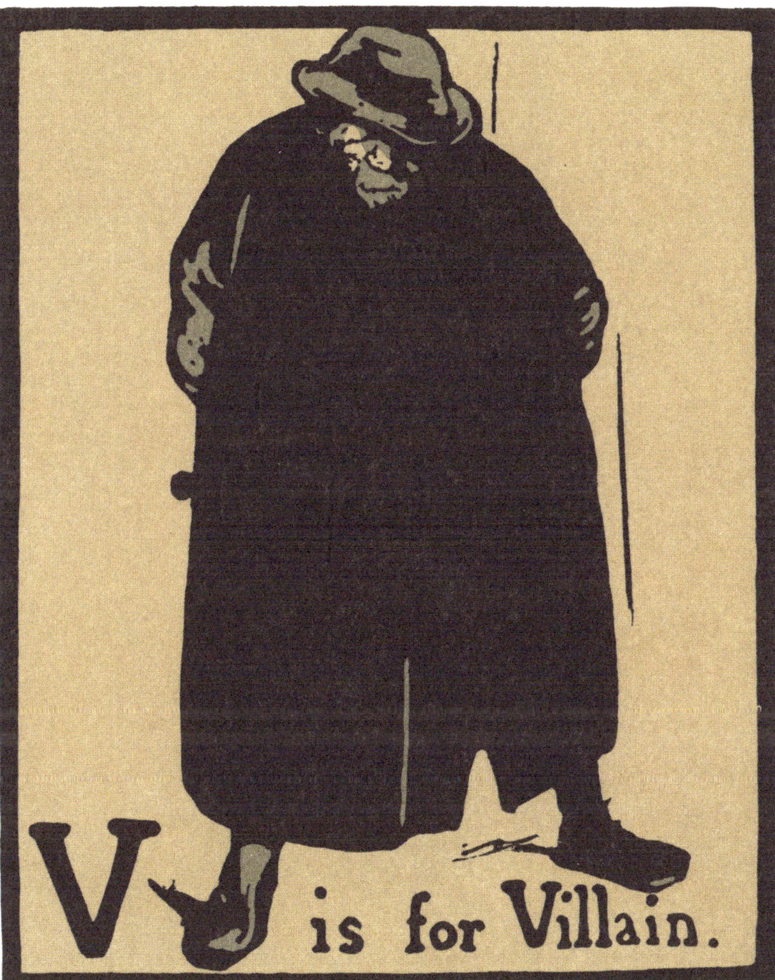
V is for Villain.

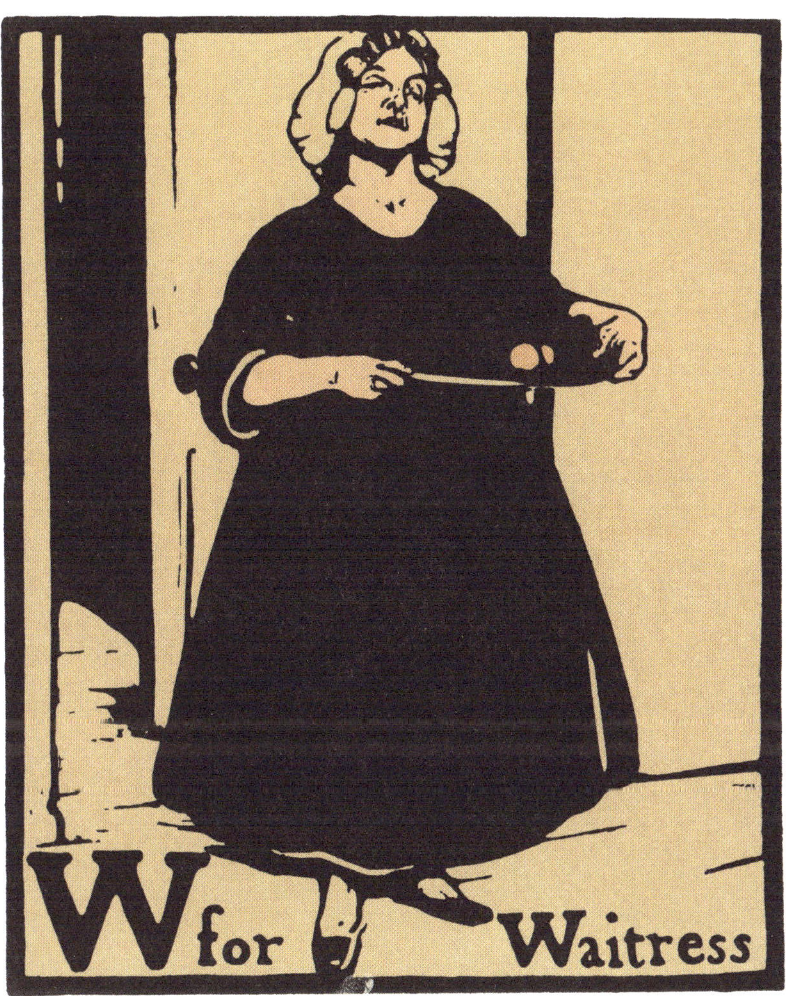
W for Waitress

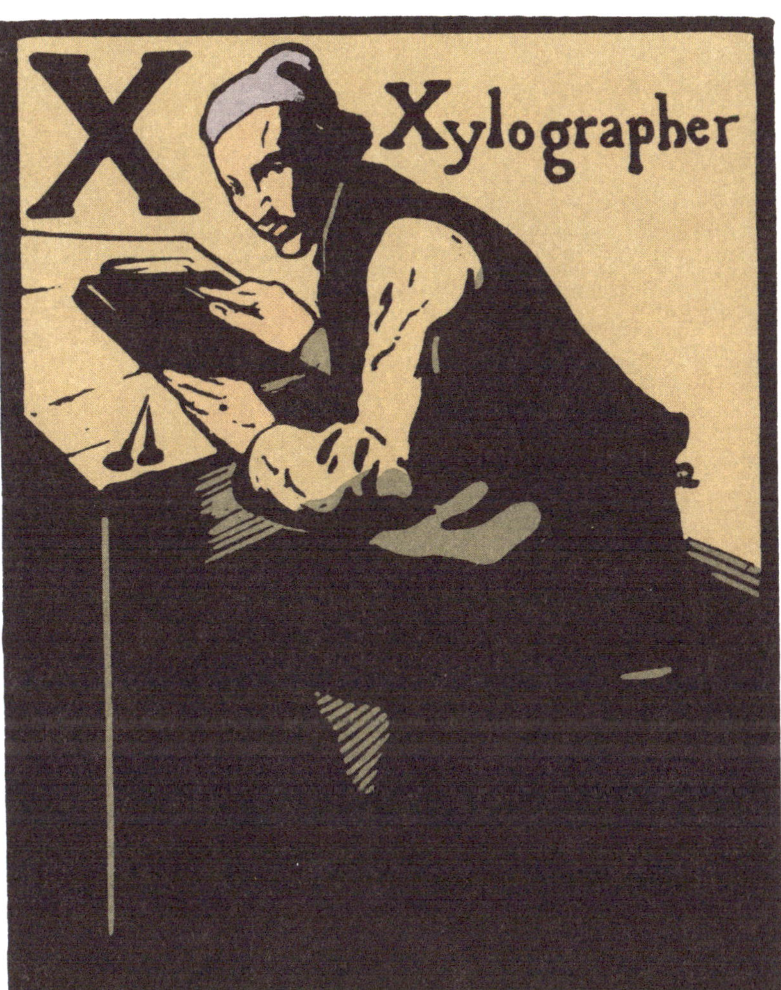
X
Xylographer

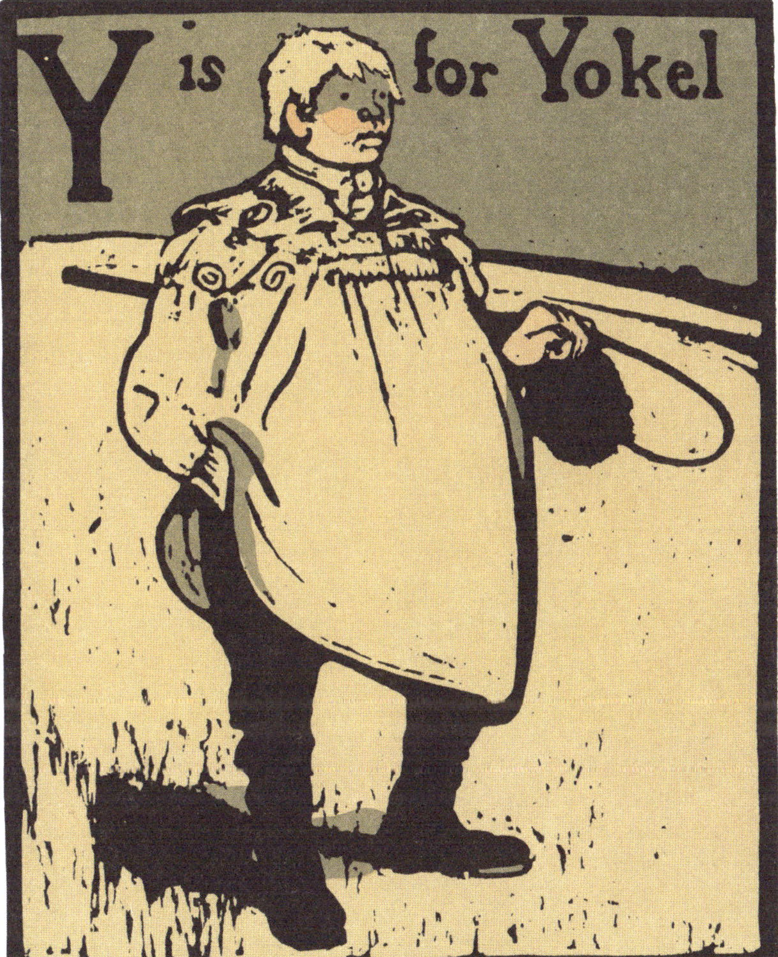
Y is for Yokel

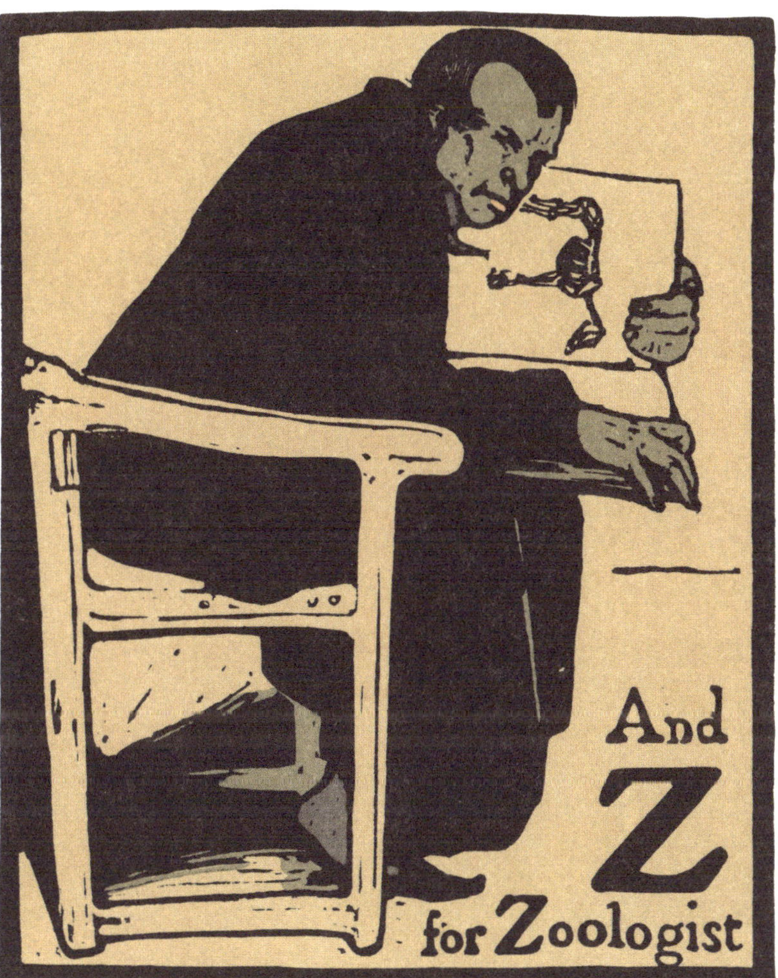
And
Z
for Zoologist

An Alphabet by William Nicholson
First published 1898 by William Heinemann
The original images measure approximately
256 x 200 mm

This edition first published 2026
by Pallas Athene (Publishers)
2 Birch Close, London N19 5XD

www.pallasathene.co.uk

Printed in China through WorldPrint

ISBN 978 1 84368 279 0